THE WOODS OF ASHRIDGE

With best wishes from Mary Blake. Aug. 2010.

POEMS

MARY BL⟨ *(obscured by barcode: GW00726705)*

THE LITTORAL PRESS

First published in 2010 by
The Littoral Press
18 Bendlowes Road
Great Bardfield
Braintree
Essex CM7 4RR

ISBN 978-0-9558937-3-5

British Library Cataloguing-in-Publication Data:
A catalogue record of this book is available from the British Library

Printed by 4edge Ltd. Hockley, Essex. www.4edge.co.uk

Contents

For

Roger Garfitt

Who opens windows

The Woods of Ashridge

In these woods all time is now,
here trees dance, cast shadows
hold secrets.
Should you pass this way
listen to the tale the trees tell.
Fox or wolf or bear,
unicorn or deer, faun or centaur.
All have entered here.

High on this northern ridge
a small stone church lost in fields,
how many cuckoo summers has it seen?
Deep in the Beechwoods, a monastery
founded on the blood of Christ
held in a crystal phial.

All this the trees know, hold
in their heartwood.
Skirting the woods, a straggly
dribble of a village
going nowhere and to everywhere.

So many pass this way: kings, saints,
pilgrims, paupers, shadows dissolve in trees.
Deep in the beechwoods bonhommes
in their robes of grey
follow the Augustinian way.

Matins at midnight, lauds in the witching hours,
prime at bird call, tierce, then sext at noon
nones at three in the afternoon, vespers at dusk,
compline, then rest. Lives lived by prayer,
the turning seasons of the year, the tolling bell.

A small breeze worries the leaves
of the sweet chestnut trees,
a row of whirling, spiralling, twisted limbs
their dancer's skirts splayed out,
their top most branches stag horned
guard the entrance with dark yews
to the monks old burial ground.
All greenness comes to withering.
Eyes watch fallow disappear as shadows
through boles of ash, of beech of sallow.

Listen with ears of heartwood, see
the confessor comes, holds
his first christ-mas, seeks solitude
after the death of his beloved Eleanor.

Below in the valley, the clerk
Geofrey Chaucer visits his old friend
John of Gaddesden, Royal Physician,
author of Rosa Angelica,
John of Gaddesden de-louser.

What of the table of silver and gold
a table to hold the cross of the True Cross
to hold the blood of Christ.
A table garnished with rubies and pearls
encrusted with sapphires and emeralds
set before the high altar.

Some say it lies buried in the woods,
the trees murmur a different tale,
spirited away by Thomas Gentleman Priest,
friend to Henry VIII last Abbot of the monastery.

Young Elizabeth by orders
of the Queen her sister, seized
from Ashridge, forced to enter
through Traitors Gate, kept close in the tower.

Time slides sideways in these woods
listen, the leaves whisper Thomas Cox
fourteen years old, he fights at Trafalgar
his ship The Colossus, he and twenty or so
powder monkeys, most perish, Thomas lives
returns to work the fields, coppice the woods
marries, lives to be the oldest man in the village.
Is that you true Thomas calling
or the leaves rap tap tapping on the window pane?

Time here is no time,
the woods remember, long ago
how the black death swept
the first village away,
houses cob walled huddled
about the church, now
only a mound shows where the windmill stood.

Shadows grow longer
remember Sin Eaters?
They took the sins of others
as their food.
"I give easement and rest now
to thee dear man, come not
down our lanes, or in our meadows
and for thy peace I pawn my own soul. Amen..."

Frost rimes the grass
a fat man with a beak of a nose
dressed in grey,
hush, don't let him hear you
Francis Duke of Bridgewater rides by
no lover of beauty he,
refused by a Gunning he swears
never to speak to a woman again
nor does he, but he builds
The Bridgewater Canal.
Father of Inland Navigation.

In these woods, all is now
what was and what is, is always.

Close to the chestnuts grow fly agaric
among spiky husks of nuts, hedgehogs
of the woods, see, small yellow
gnome like caps yellow as the yellow 'p'
stitched on paupers' sleeves.

With the closing of the monasteries
so many homeless, desperate
wanderers roam the land, seek
refuge in the woods.

Human voices calling change
to birdsong, change
to hawthorn blossom falling.

In the heartwood grows the sapling
and we shall see
the Hart who wears the Golden Chain.

Listen, on a still night
when the moon rides high
when owls cry, trees tremble,
whisper, a bat flies by, moth light
see, now mist curtains the woods.

On a still night,
should you pass this way
time becomes no time
and this is nowhere and everywhere.

Border Flowers - Flanders 15th Century

Beautiful in her smallness
soft grey as an April shower
skin, supple as a silk glove,
plump to her long tail, curled
tight, as a crescent moon.

Her hair hangs loose, cowls
her shoulders, a flower coronet
circles her head, she squats,
her breasts, quilled pink daisies,
childlike she peers

into her mirror, held
by one hand, as petals
of primrose of heartsease
speedwell and strawberry
leaves, tumble about her;

I found her in the margin
Of an old gardening book, when
sow thistles, alexanders
and colewort were grown for the pot,
almost forgotten, a mouse woman.

The Old House

He began to collect cardboard boxes
boxes of every size, he placed one up on the other
higher and higher they rose
until they filled every room,
it took a long time to cover the stairs
the landings, now the house was full

one I love, two I love
three I love I say
four I love with all my heart
five I cast away

he moved to a shepherd's hut
until that too was filled
he found a caravan, he watched
the house choke and die
fall in upon itself, smothered
by ivy, elder, cobwebs and weeds

one I love, two I love
three I love I say
four I love with all my heart
five I cast away

five caravans he filled
dress boxes, hat boxes, egg boxes
neatly stacked, his collection grew
as bindweed in a hedge
leaving no room for him

one I love, two I love
three I love I say
four I love with all my heart
five I cast away

he was found one January day
his window papered over, in his bed,
a knitted balaclava on his head
his beard spilled over his eiderdown
like a hoar frost, mittens on his hands
to keep him warm,
milk stood uncollected by his gate

one I love, two I love
three I love I say
four I love with all my heart
five I cast away

the caravans have been removed,
agents have been measuring.
The old house, the elder tree growing through its roof,
is up for auction.
They say, with the site cleared it has potential
the best view in the village,
five counties on a clear day

one I love, two I love
three I love I say
four I love with all my heart
five I cast away

odd thing is, one spot where the mist
hangs longer, where it feels cold
even in the sun,

the fox keeps clear of it
light filtering through the leaves
throws a bunch of shadows
beside a brackish pool where elderberries fall
where leaves in autumn form a mound in the soil

one I love, two I love
three I love I say
four I love with all my heart
five I cast away.

Gardens

In this row of cottages they come in all sizes
thin, wide, squat, tidy gardens, grass mown,
edges cut, hedges trim, borders bedded out,

but then, a dropped stitch a snag in the design,
exuberant old roses throwing arms in all directions
clematis intent on stars, moon gazing, draping roofs,

adorning windows, smothering chimneys, flowers
sailing skywards, honeysuckle planting flags,
flags of blossom mountaineering on the tallest trees.

Neat gardens avert their eyes, wonder at plants self sown,
long for bees for butterflies for flat red worms, notice
the heady scents, notice the birds in abundance nesting, yearn

for a garden of bird song.
Timidly they try a stray buttercup, a trail of daisies
to no avail, out come the strimmers, out come the mowers

off with their heads, nothing out of place
weed, hoe, spray, order of the day.
But on damp nights when the owl flies low

then see the slugs, giant orange ones,
pale butter yellow ones, humped back whale ones,
small thin stray grey ones,
munching lettuce, eating all they can in tidy gardens.

The untamed garden has an overgrown pond,
frogs and fat toads dine in splendour on slugs,
thrushes on snails,
flowers, shrubs, trees, expand in all their glory
for nature, as you know, grows in grandeur of decay.

Once in Mold (A Small Town in Wales)

Shrouded in mist
ground untrod
a mound to be avoided
deep in the earth
a wonder hid.
Gold under gravel
gone to earth.

Delicate as hoarfrost
a shawl of gold,
necklace of amber
a hoard untold
four thousand years old.
Gold under gravel
gone to earth.

Note: Beowulf
They let the ground keep
that Ancestral Treasure.
Gold under gravel, gone to earth.

Wednesday

Nothing unusual about the day.
Robins singing, birds busy
among holly berries,
deer across the path in the bracken
browsing.
Hard frost rimes the grass
so sharp the air it pierces
my cheek, a shining winters day.
There he was,
leaning on my gate
a slouched, soft brimmed
hat shading his face,
covering one eye, there by my gate.
Strangers seldom pass this way
"Come in" I said,
but he was gone, leaving
only his footprints sparkling
on the frost,
a man who paused a while
then faded in the shadows of the wood,
a man of stars, two black crows
flying about his head, whispering in his ear,
It was Wednesday.

Sounds of the Sea

Sounds of the sea, of a shingle beach,
footsteps at night crunching the pebbles,
smell of tar, feel of tar, of wrack,
marram grass growing, swaying, hiding
children playing, playing houses.

Boom of the fog horn blowing
small fingers knitting scarves,
knitting balaclava helmets
for the sailors of the Girldler's Lightship
out in all weathers, sea tossing.

Watching the light at night, wash
my walls white, lulling me to sleep.

Sand gardens, sand castles, sand
in our sandwiches, between toes
under fingernails, in our bed sheets.

Below the old pier, our woollen swimsuits
hung out to dry, baggy to our knees,
rock, pink and white, sweet to suck,
rock pools to cool our feet, crabs to catch
star fish, wanting to be a mermaid,
my first disappointment.

Morning

Four o'clock on a summer's morning
moth-light on the silent garden,
no breeze stirs leaves or trees
listening for that first bird clinking
slicing of silence.

Answering the one bird
comes another, then another,
I can't distinguish blackbird
from mistle thrush, I hear
the deep throated ring dove all sky
jingling,
my world explodes in sound, a huge wave
gathering force, pounding cliffs, booming
through caves, layer upon layer of song
surfeiting reverberating,
sonorous as creations dulcimer.
For this precious half hour
I am woven into bird's song, a fledgling
learning to fly, a feather floating
until, suddenly as it began   it is stilled
I am left with my neighbours unsettling
cockerel with three black ruffian raucous crows flapping
firmly to earth me.

Unable to Walk on Pavements

Mermaids seldom walk in woods
if not sea, they need grass underfoot,
soft rain upon the face, need
to watch the turning of the year.

Unable to walk on pavements
placed in a city or a town,
mermaids wither to a whisper.

Best at making fragrant flower crowns,
sea lavender, sea blackthorn, love in the mist
freely given, freely received.

They ask for little, to make their bread,
their soup, be part of moon and stars.
Deep in their head they hear the song of whales,
but have grown accustomed to the song of birds.

Carry them gently back to the sea
while there is time, place on their tongues
the thin wafer, the sign of the fish,
allow them to eat silence.

I can't Remember now if it was May

Sent into Somerset in November
from a city hung in elephants
soft grey barrage balloons, of sandbagged trenches,
gas masks, the blackout.
A shy frightened child who couldn't cry
who watched the Thames on fire.

I can't remember now if it was May,
a small town by the sea, white thatched
cob cottages, a harbour wall,
the Minehead hobby horse, excitement in the air.

Two men under a spotted canvas skin
a great horse's wooden head,
eyes that rolled, tongue that lolled bright red.
A wild horse prancing, menacing, dancing,
sent us screaming, half in terror, wanting,
hoping to be caught, somewhere with pipe and drum
a fiddle played.

What is Safe?

We seemed safe from the war
our teachers played us Bach,
madrigals I'd never heard.
Herbs and flowers were everywhere,
we lived by festivals, Halloween, Advent,
our present from our teachers,
the ancient Mystery Plays.
St John's fire that had to be out by dusk,
boys jumped over the flames.

Miss Mellon had the sweetest,
pale blue eyes, was round and plump and soft,
she wove her own clothes on a handmade loom,
other teachers painted, carved, we children
weeded, hoed, planted by the moon
stirred compost with a cow's horn.

Only nothing is safe.
Cocooned in this web of beauty, too soon
dark fingers began their strangler's hold,
an older boy in the class above, riding
his bicycle too fast was killed, we children
found a different route to school.

Some parents were interned and class mates
visited the Isle of Man, Werner Thurau, Heinz,
Eva Frömmer, her crippled brother,
nothing was ever said.

A teacher's son reported missing, lost at sea
presumed drowned, Captain Field was ill for a week.

A crashed plane, the pilot dead, the smell
of oil, of burning filled our throats,
our nostrils, even while we dreamed.

Before the Glass Cracks

We that live on remember
those who journey far into the unknown.
Our friends, our loves still fill our rooms, sit
on our chairs, their words in our ears
see, only a hand's span, fingertip away.
Quietly some vanish
as foam on the rocks,
you Anna Akhmatova sear
our thoughts, burn into our minds
little convict woman,
we are the samphire gatherers
we watch for black sails,
gatherers of drift wood, of dross.
Shall we recognise the messenger
will he stand four square
or a shadow glimpsed in the mirror
before the glass crazes and cracks,
a familiar voice calling us home
as the sparrow-hawk claims his fledgling
or the vixen cries in the night
we return to the earth,
have you noticed
the smile on a skull?

Cast Iron Flowers

In the corner of a derelict vicarage garden
among old bicycle wheels, broken kettles,
cast iron flowers push from brambles, nose
through tall nettles as salmon leap upstream
or an old ship's prow parts water;
cast iron ends of a Victorian seat
restored now, it rests beneath my apple tree
here primroses grow, a garden of old fashioned flowers,
sweet William, Hattie's pincushion, old laced pinks
love-in-the-mist.
Deer come at night drink from the pool
frogs sit motionless as stone.
A quiet place where a thought could grow.

Thread (A Sequence)

As if looking
through the wrong end
of old fashioned binoculars
I see myself, a child
arms held out
my aunt unravels
a jersey, I watch the garment
shrivel, nothing wasted.
The skeins washed, hung to dry,
looped as frizzy hair.
My aunt, as did Penelope
picks up her needles,
skeins become balls of wool
a new garment in the making.
The sound of my childhood
the click of her needles.

Mr Grandfather the Doctor
was a collector of charms
the old ways long forgotten.
In Galway as a boy,
he remembered folk
coming to the house
praying for the "cure"
seven hundred years
a mere nothing
in a family's memory
and he,
the son of the Lady of the cure.
What's that you say
who was the lady, what was the cure?
A thread from a handkerchief

once dipped in the blood
of King Charles I,
and the Lady?
St Margaret of Scotland
the charm to cure scrofula,
tubercular swellings,
Kings evil
Can you beat that?

On New Year's Eve
who brought in
The Flower of the Well?
Spill not a drop
the pitcher
must not touch the ground.
In every room sprinkle
the clear water
sing Levy dew, sing Levy dew
the water and the wine.
Who put the holly wreath
around the horse's neck?
who nailed the holly
to the cattle shed door
keeping the beasts from harm?
As puffs of smoke
fade and are no more
or thistledown on the air
foam on the breakers blown willy-nilly
not known where,
for so short a time, we are here
then gone.

Walking in the woods
thinking of Zac
a grandson lost
never to know old age,
today is his birthday
I walk to his oak tree
my gentle giant,
marvel how the oak has grown.
The silver birches
have shed their leaves,
the beech golden
only the oaks
still hold their green.
How still the wood
no nightingales,
a friendly robin sings
in the far distance the sound of traffic
above is the roar of a plane,
as far as I can see
bracken the colour of fox.

Pull the bobbin pull the bobbin
pull, pull, pull

Needles and pins, needles and pins
shall I shorten my garment
or as my aunt
undo and remake?
Is our life one long
making and remaking,
patching and darning
shreds and tatters.
What of La Blaca, the black one
who came so long ago

out of Wales with the Normans
was he black in countenance or deeds?
What of Walter, smothered
in a feather bed, the cure
three hundred years ago
for hydrophobia, better than
rabies.
By the end of his centenary
the family money was squandered,
as wild geese flown.
What of my grandfather Marlay
rich in leech lore, rich
in the blarney, in Brehon Law.
Did the gift rest on him,
son of the Lady of the cure?
What of Leo my father awarded
the Military Cross in 1918,
"he displayed great courage
and skill in attending
to the wounded at all hours,
night and day."
Leo, the doctor, did it rest,
the gift on him?
Now Tamara,
my granddaughter the doctor
will the gift come to her?
So many patterns, so many
variations, one gift
given so long ago, one thread
Surely, we grow tall
on the shoulders of our ancestors.

Before the War

Its nineteen thirty six
Hark the herald angels sing
Mrs Simpson stole our King,
I'm at the hut down on the beach
the smell of seaweed, seabirds crying,
I'm watching Aunt Mary dancing,
the wind-up gramophone plays
I love my chilli bom bom
my chilli bom bom loves me.
Aunt Mary wears white bell bottom trousers
smokes her black cigarette
in a long amber holder
paints her nails red.
I wish I wore high heeled
open sandals, mine are dull
dark brown, brown as mud, 'Startrite',
I wish my hair would curl
like Aunt Mary.
Mothers of my school friends
hardly ever swim, wear buns
wear sensible shoes,
their girls wear liberty bodices,
my friend Gwendoline Crump
wears a liberty bodice,
Aunt Mary says its very old fashioned,
Gwendoline takes home her bodice
in a brown paper bag,
Gwendoline doesn't play with me anymore.
Aunt Mary has a steel six inch hat pin
she keeps I under pillow,
Aunt Mary places pepper pots
beside our front door,

Aunt Mary says, she's not afraid to use them
shows me how
life is very safe with Aunt Mary,
that is, it was before the war,
Hark the herald angels sing
Mrs Simpson's stole our King

A Thin Place

A thin place
walking the woods
or high on the Beacon,

once by Horner waters
in the shallows
where fingers can change to minnows
feet slip on stepping stones
become lilies,

where a moment
stretches, cobwebs a whole life
resounds as a Buddhist's bell

childhood to old age in an instant
the smell of darkness, of dampness
feel of moss, sounds of water

a thin place.

Tidal Waters

As a child, I slept
to the sounds of the sea
with unknown footsteps
beneath my window

My window, a prow
of an old sailing ship.
Shingle as far as I could see
grey skies, grey shingle, grey sea.

Scrunch of deep pebbles above water line.
No trees, a harshness, rocks, gulls are flowers.
Sloshing, spewing of sea and spray
against harbour walls and quay.

Night brings the boom of the light ship
light washes my walls white
a comfort in the mournful moan of fog horn.
Westcliff and Eastcliff.

A quiet bay with the ruins of Reculver
two crumbling towers looking out to sea.
We children would climb and peer through narrow slits,
pretend we searched the waves for Danes.

All we saw were shadows
faintly on the horizon,
as if pencilled in,
large ocean going tankers.

Westcliff was near the pier
visitors, trippers
here was the train station
close to the charabanc yard.

Vacancy signs hung
in net curtained windows
rude postcards and sweet
long thin sticks of rock.

Fat men paddled
their trousers rolled about their knees
handkerchief tied about bald heads
was it children or the gulls that screamed?

Eastcliff was where we lived
but barbed wire came
soldiers came.
No longer were the beach, the cliffs, our playground.

War came, we moved to London,
bombs came, eyeless houses
gutted houses, rotted rubble
trenches were dug in the High Street.

I longed for small woods, the softness
of dew ponds, primroses, lily of the valley,
farmyards, not air raid shelters,
cockerels crowing, warm eggs newly laid.

Sent out of London to Somerset,
here there was still sea,
gentle sea where woods
tumbled down hills to silent creeks.

Here were farmyards,
we woke to cock call
the smell of new milled corn, fresh milk
bread baking, ciders fermenting.

Cottages were thatched
their honeyed walls wattle and daub.
We were cocooned, small chrysalises
swaying on our twigs, waiting to emerge.

Many years later
married with a young son
living in London, I met an old lady,
I told her how I longed for the country

It will happen my dear, she said,
if you want something that badly
it always will.
I hadn't seen her wand.

Feast Day

Four cow bells by my door
their metal tongues
shining with frost
winter's crown imperials.

Holly trees in threes
lean over the barn
terracotta tiles
quicken to silver fishes.

On the broad hedge
two robins dance
stick legged, currant eyed.

Today is the feast
of Saint Bride
tomorrow Candlemas.

On the dark earth
one white feather
lights the garden.

Candles

When I was a child
far from bombs
birthdays at school
were special.
In that darkness
our birthday candle
shone tall and bright
spluttering in a draught
rising and falling as shadows
danced on the wall.
At the table, our place
decorated
with wild flowers, berries and twigs.
For a day
we were the chosen one, the appointed,
Jubilate, no need for us to wear a crown.

When in midwinter
my grandson
in his open coffin lay
amidst flowers in the hall
a tall candle by his head
I sat and stroked his hair
he wasn't there, he
had become as marble.
So many years ago
still each day, in the hall
they light a candle.
He was the chosen one, no
Jubilate, we wear the willow
Zac it is who wears the crown.

Four candles on the Advent wreath,
as children we went to the forest
collected our fire, our cones,
our class room smelt of pine.
The wreath hung by red ribbon,
four red candles, one for each week
until all four were lit.
Under the wreath we sang our carols,
The holly and the ivy, in the bleak midwinter,
safe in Somerset
while bombs were falling, and we sang
how we sang.
Jubilate, no need for us to wear a crown.

Candlemas, festival of light,
light in our darkness.
Bridget, patron saint
of small animals, of creatures lost,
of poets.
Midwinter as the snowdrop pierces the dark earth,
the chosen one, the appointed,
Jubilate, no need for us to wear a crown.

On grass hills the hares are boxing,
pussy willow for Palm Sunday, for Christ's scourge.
"Ellem do grieve
oak he do hate
willow do walk
if you travels late."
Pussy willow, fluffy yellow goslings,
wood of the gallows.
We light our candle,
Here is the chosen one, the appointed
the shape shifter.

Jubilate, no need for us to wear a crown.

Cry ho the Lent lily, the daffodil snow,
light the Easter candle,
the pasque flower its bright green
dye to stain our Easter eggs,
jam jars filled with primroses,
primrose balls to swing on a cow's tail,
now no witch can pass.
For primrose is the chosen one, the appointed
Jubilate, no need for us to wear a crown.

Come celebrate
all living things,
the chosen, the appointed,
now is the time all wear the crown
sun, moon, stars and planets,
light all our candles, sing loud hosanna, sing
Jubilate, Jubilate, wood louse and snail,
Jubilate to the fieldmouse, butterfly and wren.

Ivinghoe

From nowhere
we were among them.
As far as I could see
ragged, woolly ,
enormous Chiltern sheep.
As if we were surrounded by clouds, no
in clouds,
our car drove sheep pace.
Have you been in a wood
when without warning,
an old tree lets fall a limb?
The very air, even the grass,
aware, expectant, no birds sing.
It was the same with the sheep,
one moment, so many,
then as if they heard
what we couldn't hear, they parted,
these great sheep clouds
rolled slowly down the valley
leaving us
an empty road, overhung
by ancient beeches,
below us
stretched five counties.
Such a gift to be given,
alive in a Samuel Palmer painting.

Summer Storm

On the edge of the wood
pale hands, elder flowers
finger each leaf.
Here trees dance,
their great limbs
sway, hold up the sky.
Yolk yellow, wild
azaleas, spider flowers
scent the air.

In the garden
garnered by the rain,
each shrub, bush,
heavy as a wooden barque
hunkers down
waiting to be bailed.
Flowers lie dismayed
broken, bruised, limp
strewn across the grass.
Parched earth quenched
the water butt overflows,
on the window of the cottage
snails trail paths of silver.

February

Snowflakes whiffling down
as winter geese
feathering fields, woods, gardens,

nesting on all it touches
transforming ugliness, only arrow scratches,
trail of birds feet, footprint of deer of fox

disturb this hushed world, a world
where shadows bruised blue, cast
nets, snares in soft unbroken snow

a noose for the unwary, to sink
silently, muffled in webs of frozen lace
snow on snow,

devouring silence, concealed
under white wings
under a crescent moon, Brigid's goslings.

A Small Death

Bent as I was on clearing
corn cockle, red campion,
over blown cranesbill,
snip, snip, my eyes devouring
yet more straggling flowers,
I never saw him, an extra snip,
so valiantly he struggled
alive, but cut clean in half.
I could not bear his agony
I took a heavy stone
ended his small life.

All that day long I could not garden.
A frog who went a-wooing,
heigh ho says Rowley,
not even a duck to gobble him up,
just me, poor frog, your nemesis.

My Party Frock

is white organdie, edged
with pale primroses
and a stiff broad satin
sash

my collar scratches
my small puff sleeves
are a little tight,
I won't sit, in case

I spoil my frock, crush
the satin bow
tied at my back.
I am wearing petticoats

and my knickers match.
Why do the children stare
I don't understand
the words they speak,

we are all strangers
in this house, uncertain
fearful of shadows, of dry
leaves tapping at the window.
It is September 1939.

Pebble

Small grey pebble, water worn
I hold you in my hand
a world, a globe, a sphere
I close my fist
you disappear
open, a universe
where giants hurtle rocks,
sucked into waters you fell,
were fashioned, appear.
The Devil spat
causeways erupt
shimmering as eels
forests grew
tidal waters break
nothing is as it seems
all is growth and change,
refrain expanding into song
listen,
one bird, now another
until the sky reverberates
louder and louder,
louder than waves breaking against rocks
as if to drown
not in flowers- as is my custom-
not in the grey wet widow maker
fishes for lovers,
but in the chorus of the dawn
you and I pebble
we shall fly.

Magnolia Grandiflora

So many ladybirds looking for a safe winter home
basking in late October sun
sparkling on shiny green magnolia leaves
leaves like small children's feet
brown soles soft as velvet
small jewelled ladybirds, pins for a fine lady to wear.

The strange fruit of the flower
a miniature pineapple in shades of grey and green,
the dry dead leaves rustle, do not fall
feel like old leather on a well worn high backed library chair
or the cover of old forgotten books,
a few of last year's leaves hang hidden on the wall, faded to pale
cinnamon.

In the night, when the wind blows softly
the leaves tell another story, listen
small children's feet running,
frightened, hidden, soles of their feet bleeding
looking for sanctuary,
whispers remembered in magnolia leaves
strange fruit hanging in the trees.

Handstaff of Holly

Cobwebs net the bushes
as a snood nets a girl's hair,
silent the woods in mist
night brings the rut of deer
call of owl,
day folded on oyster sky
branches sparkle
dew dropped as moonstones
in this mushroom softness of early autumn.

Past now the shortest day,
past the hunting of the wren.
A knight, a crippled one, long gone
lives in a hall, of his wounds
doth bleed both day and night.
At that bed's head there grows a thorn.
In slipper green spring has come
frost and snow departed
bleak winds no longer blow
blackbird and thrush are singing.

Deeper in the woods
shadows walk between the oaks.
How the earth turns, surely
the Fisher King has passed this way,
St Mark's Gowk sings summer in,
paigles, St Peter's keys cover the hill,
woodsmoke in the valley
pale anemones star the forest floor
scent of bluebells washes the air,
the cuckoo calls,
I follow, my handstaff of holly before me.

Wooden Wheel

This is my spoked wooden wheel
handcrafted, turned, made from the heartwood.
I hang it with mistletoe, hoarfrost
flowers of blackthorn, may blossom, dew.

One spoke is made from baby's breath
      milk warm with lullabies, with pain,
one spoke oiled with herb of grace, pungent
      a salve for neighbours.
One spoke is mossed, soft, smelling of whortleberries,
      of seaweed, a pool in Horner Waters
      reflecting faces of long ago friends.
One spoke for Tom the Post, soft voiced as smoke soon
      to retire as letters are few as winter leaves
      who will bring gossip not that empty mouthed box
      haw red and peeling, close to the woods.
One spoke for Dick, round as a dumpling, organic carrots
      bunched in his arms, smelling of tee tree,
      Yoga and Zen.
One spoke for Harry, hunched in all weathers, silently
      slips as a fox through my gate in brown leather
      gaiters smelling of earth-mould, leaves milk on my step.
One spoke moon washed, sun bleached, hung with fragile lanterns
      beacons in the darkness for Madingley poets.
This is my wheel for the winds to turn, a spinning wheel
      wheel within wheel for my hands to hold.

Portrait of an Englishwoman
(By Hans Holbein the Younger)

Lady, who are you?
you, with so much sadness in your eyes.
Drawn by a Master in red and black chalk
such delicate eyebrows.
Perhaps from the Court of Henry V111?
Tell me, were you aware of all those intrigues?
Is that why your eyes hold secrets?
I hope that your days at Court were few,
that you married well,
tended your herbs and simples,
lesser celandine to purify the blood,
meadow clary to clear the sight,
fernseed to make you invisible.
Unknown lady, so much sadness in your eyes
it pervades the centuries.
Still, you hold your secrets.

Markers

Magical
mystical
mathematical
being
bringing forth
growth
harmony
with earth
with spirit
Plato
Copenicus
Tycho Brahe.

Anagallis Arvensis

On my wall
a stick barometer,
in the garden
slender, small,
scarlet star face
intent on sky worship
creeps prostrate,
closes petals
as clouds hide sun.
Scarlet pimpernel
cousin to the poppy,
shepherds sundial
poor man's weatherglass,
John-go-to-bed-at-noon.
For Gerard said,
"No heart can think
no tongue can tell
the virtues
of the pimpernel."

Warning

Was it soft September
when the earliest of apples,
Beauty of Bath are ripe,
or, when the first leaves
fall, when mists hide the valley
when rutting deer are heard?

Slowly at first
this infestation,
I hardly noticed.
Not the usual webs
but slender wisps
a snuffed out candle leaves
or goose grass catching at your legs.

In every room, under chairs,
from lamps, festooned from doors
wisps fine as spun silk.
Small parcels neatly wrapped
under the long case clock
far from the broom, wood lice
packed bundles stored for food.

No ordinary spider this,
not the large fast moving black
who loves the moisture of the sink,
this spider is fragile, delicate
as a lace wing, a survivor.
Once, she wove to out-weave Hera,
Arachne is revenged, lives in our row of cottages.
Watch when you sleep tonight
she does not weave your shroud.

Marjorie Kempe - Born 1373

Icicles hang from the thatch
from the windows of the solar,
death and famine stalk the land
I wait to see my celandine unfold
then about my business,
my path is not an easy one
no primroses but thistles, ruts and mire.

They say
I was seized with madness
after my first born babe,
it is no madness
unless to serve my God is mad,
I go about his work
it is not easy to be chosen
to dress in white

pierced by such a sacred love
I am his creature.

Satan, do your worst, your whisperings
always in my head
this freshet's finger scratching, dribbling
slithering honey in my ears,
if fourteen babes can not hold me
what hope hast thou?
I tussle with the dark one every hour of every day.

I go lusting for my God
in a swirl of dust
I beat the drum, call my wares
beset by every peril
tested to breaking
no sea too perilous
even unto Danzig.

His creature knows no humiliation.
I crawl in dust, eat dirt
even unto Santiago.
Sinners repent, the hour is near.
In Canterbury they call me Lollard
crowds chase me through the streets
took me to burn.

I shall tie me to this tree,
This post, no man stop my mouth,
Not my father, John Brunham or Bishop's Lynn
Six times Member of Parliament,
Justice of the peace, Chamberlain;
Not John, my Goodman, shadow of my father
he has our children, he worries over debts.

Though tears wash my cheeks
my hands, my breasts,
I am canny with our money
God whispers in his creature's ear.
I am about his work, to roam,
to Assisi, to the Holy Land
to fight the Infidel.

My Pilgrim's shell I wear
my cloak of dun
my broad brimmed hat
my staff; no path too long
no voyage too turbulent,
a white moth on his breath I flutter,
his creature.   Repent while there is time.

My Goodman John, his love is carnal
he would wrestle hold me safe at home,
I am sworn God's creature only.
Repent ye sinners while there is time,
And yes, I miss our younglings, miss sweet smelling hay,
Fresh milk, the daisies by my door,
I am sworn God's creature, I ask no more.

The Rhythm of Life is a Powerful Thing

You were born in Hammersmith hospital.
I didn't know then, it overlooked
Wormwood Scrubs, a sad place,
what a way to come into life
you who love the out of doors,
who are never still
even now, grown up, a middle aged
mother of four, how hard it is
for you to be still,
not like me, your mother,
I can sit for hours just gazing at clouds.
My mornings have become later and later
you are up by seven,
dogs walked, horses watered,
you walk at a run, I amble
do you ever draw breath?
My body is spreading, fingers thicken,
you the greyhound, the hare,
I the tortoise.
Keep up, keep up, you cry
as we walk the fields
I've stopped, lost in the beauty of hawthorn blossom
I'm counting daisies to see if spring has come,
for the sight of red kite flying.
You can wash your hair, bake a cake
iron the clothes in the time it takes me
just to feed the chickens, and I'm getting slower.
Once it was learning to dance,
quick step, slow, slow, slower.
You so tall and slim
I am getting smaller, rounder
pretty good for cuddles.

Something has changed,
this time in hospital
you were so good and caring,
we've changed places
I was once the carer,
its come full circle,
O the rhythm of life is a powerful thing.

…And Eva Pleasured Adam

When I was a child of seven or more,
I lived in a house with a stout oak door,
my bed was soft, with a sycamore floor.
With a hey down, derry down, derry down daw.

The apple-tree danced till her roots were sore, were sore.

When I was a girl of twelve or more,
our house exploded, it was the second world war,
nothing was left but a smear on the floor, the floor.
With a hey down, derry down, derry down daw.

It's the way of the world, child, the pear-tree knew more.

When I was young, say twenty four,
like a rose I bloomed, two blossoms bore,
but love was lost, like a mouse in the straw, the straw.
With a hey down, derry down, derry down daw.

The blackthorn sighed, she'd heard it before, before

I've lived and I've loved; now winter winds roar,
hail beats at my window, rain through the cracks pour.
If an apple is rotten, it's black to the core, the core.
With a hey down, derry down, derry down daw.

Yet the apple's heart, the plum tree replies, is a golden star.

If you're looking for love, plant an orchard of trees,
apple, pear, sloe, plum for blossom and bees,
delighting all creatures, whatever they be.
With a hey down, derry down, derry down daw.

If it's pleasuring your seeking, you'll find it for sure.

Water Lily

Crushed between his fingers, such a small fragment
limp as her small body, face down, arms spread
as a water lily, as if she were watching fish far
below, but floating

a fragment from her dress, how? He did not know,
he should have tried harder to catch her running
so alive through the grasses, her laughter lost
in the sound of rooks returning in the evening.

Daddy watch me, watch me, he hears her in the rain
in the wind, in the leaves, Daddy watch me
he hears her in the sound of traffic, watch me
in the steam of the kettle, the scratching
of birds in the eves early,

Emily aged seven, Emily of those strong limbs
fingers beginning to change from little child
to girl but never woman,
hands eager for making music, for drawing.

Eyes not grey, a hint of blue as his Norfolk skies
like the sheen on the lake.
In the sound of rooks he had not heard the splash
as his daughter floated

caught not by his hands, caught in the end by reeds,
holding her close to warm her, not believing what his eyes
what his heart told him, keening her name, rocking
backwards and forwards, with the rooks calling.

Now in the cool of evening he walks this path
through the long grasses, remembering,
his new neighbour by the lake fishing, unknowing,
looks up smiling, hearing the rooks.

Backwater

A row of cottages
higgledy piggeldy
some squat as a toad, some
lighthouse tall, tumbled together
as though a horny handed gardener
had dropped beans and where
they fell, cottages had grown.
Hidden by briar, woodbine, ivy,
from unwanted eyes,
here spindle berries, sugar almonds of the hedge
spit their pink,
only wood-smoke whispers cottages are here,
close by the woods.
White clouds scud, sailing
fast across the sky
fat as fleecy sheep.

Cottage windows glint
trawl moon, or sun, or stars.
Turn around
you might find
an ancient beech or oak
dance, in this burnt sugar light
of autumn, a measured La Volta,
turn widdershins,
only a slight movement in the leaves
a stillness of shadows
shows where the dance has been.

Liloceris Lilii (*All curses are to my knowledge authentic Old Irish*)

Red lily beetle, curses on you
beautiful though you are
with your scarlet body, slim and long,
your black head, black legs,
devourer of my lilies.
May you be broken over the mason's cliff.
Woe to you,
dirty fellow you've filthied me.
May hound-wounding vultures gouge your eyes.
Rain and fire, ill wind, snow,
hard frost follow you.
You are not one of us, our summer's warmer
you flew the channel, decided you would stay.
The devil sweep you sideways.
May the entrails and mansion of pleasure
of this worm fall out.
Red lily beetle
your young disgust me,
dirty orange-red, fat with humps
with black heads, cover themselves
in their own slimy excreta.
Out from my garden, out I say.
The devil sweep you,
the devil swallow you sideways.
From March to October, you marauding pirates
you pillage, suck dry my lilies,
Worse than the plagues of Egypt I give you,
I give you red lily beetle, I give you to the devil
May the devil cut the head off you
and make a day's work of your neck.
Bad cess to you, boil in damnation, red lily beetle.

A Man

I met him once, twice perhaps,
a viola player.
I remember his hands,
his voice a choral,
his eyes swallowed you.

In a concentration camp
with friends, they played
Bach, Mozart, Brahms.
After the war, still together
they formed a quartet.

I would listen on my radio.
A sudden heart attack the announcer said,
I felt as if someone close to me had died.

I met his wife,
said how sad his loss.
Surprised she looked at me
yes she said, he died.
There was no warmth
no friendship in her eyes.

On Reading Rosamond Lehmann's Last Testament - 1982

Like Rosamond Lehmann I too
am in my eighty-first year
and yes, it is more than likely
I am on the last stage of my journey.

Conceived in Baghdad, born in Somerset,
a cold winter in 1928 when snow
a foot deep or more lasted well into April
when water in jugs in bedrooms froze solid.

I remember a London garden
where you walked through lawns,
down steep steps into a secret place.

I was three years old,
elves and fairies I knew
lived here, among the flowers and the butterflies.

Now it is the woods where I find peace,
peace in my cottage,
my garden never has lost its magic.

In the woods, the great oaks, the ancient beeches
here wild honeysuckle climb tall trees
ivy hangs in swags, all in enchantment.

Time slides sideways or stands still,
shadows of the quick and dead hold hands
Romans, Saxons, monks, knights, pedlars,

They say the blackbird was the Druid's sacred bird,
the wren, the robin, birdsong at dawn,
to the starlings black fishnet clouds as they prepare
for night, I feel part of, protected by, nature.

At one with badger, fox, deer, the fieldmouse
bats even the old rat, are we not
all part of this amazing burgeoning earth?

Yes, I wonder more often now how death will come,
when, how it will be, I have seen so much of death,
shall I be aware when my time comes to fade into nature?

I, who when young was immortal, how many moons
shall I watch rise and wane, give me ten more springs,
ten more snows, too soon it is all passed,
now watch the stars grow near.

I who am part of all those, those who have already been,
my father, grandfathers, mother, grandmothers,
way, way back to those early Celts.

Now I watch my grandchildren, blown as dandelion clocks
out into their new world, you do not expect
to out live your young, an agony hard to understand.

The bud becomes the flower, the flower
sets seed and falls, leaving only its shadow,
but the seed to fall before the bloom, that is hard.

My maiden Aunt, who after caring for my mother,
after my mother's death, became my guardian,
what, aunt, do you think of this world?

You who saw the death of Queen Victoria, the Boer war,
nursed in world war one and two, saw the Empire
you loved, were so proud of, fall, India torn in two.

Saw the first man land on the moon, aunt, so much
change in so few years, sad you never knew
my children's children, all is ephemeral, nothing stays,

only perhaps great trees, the oaks, the yews
the Druid's knew, the holly bough of Chaucer
I still hand, decorate with candles each Christmas still,

hold hands across the years with those long gone,
wonder if in the dusk about my cottage or
sitting by my fire are the shades of those I've loved and lost.

I feel closer now to them, than those
I see each day, yet loving every moment of what
I am given, greedy for more.

Thinking of that old lady who
in the dark of winter
in her favourite chair
sat planning next years flower border

a neighbour called, the following day,
she was still in her chair
her packets of seed laid out before her,
now, there's a way to go.

Winter

Dark the woods, dark the trees
snow outlines branches
as chalk on a school blackboard.
Birds silent, search for food,
ice holds the earth
and yet,
in this sea of cold, birds still fly
fly from frozen bush to bush.
A blackbird scurries down the path
souls so small
how do you survive?
The barn door ajar,
some protection from winter's blast.

Stranger at the Door

You wrote my name upon the sand
the waters washed away this hand
you never came by sea or land.
Who is this stranger at my door?
Too late dear shadow, man of straw
all my ears hear is never more.
Your smile too stretched, your collar worn
your hair too long a sight forlorn
too late, too late the past is gone,
you who could charm a rattle snake
a sorry sight dear heart you make,
don't blame this love for your mistake,
a card or two came through the post
I don't know what I miss the most
you the hero, or you dear ghost?
I still exist, and you… almost.

Dalliance with a Plant

Beside black hollyhock
candles of verbascum,
an explosion of blossom
hummock of stars
nectar for hoverflies,
sea foam that Aphrodite
might appear from,
a haze of gypsophila.
Wanton creature
you have me in your thrall
you tease and beguile me,
here you flourish
with me you will not grow.
Capricious as ever
I shall try and forget you
until,
unexpected
I walk in some garden
and there in full glory,
a crinoline of guipure lace
a mantilla of white
I am undone.

Nightingale at Madingley

In May, at Madingley, I woke to hear
a song so clear, so pure, pure as a mountain beck
long and intricate and can I say mathematic,
which for me is strange, who still counts on fingers and thumbs.

In July, at Madingley, in the quiet of the night
again this song so near, a gift not looked for,
"To cease upon the midnight with no pain
while thou art pouring forth thy soul abroad."

Never have I heard a nightingale , of course
it had to be a man to break the spell,
"you heard a robin, they sing all night, don't you read the
Telegraph?"

He's wrong; I heard a nightingale, a flute, a waterfall of sound

Even if I never hear the song again,
To have known it once, is enough
I shall carry in my ears for as long as I live
this glorious, *kleine nacht* music.

December 21st

Do not place stones in my pocket
nor whistle over grey waters
I hear well enough the plash of oars;

in the subtle colours of winter
spring is Eastering forth,
silent the wood, a few oaks

still hold their tissue umber leaves;
high on a branch a magpie
feathered in clerical black and white

watches and waits; a beached
midwinter sun peers through bare
branches from a shot silk sky;

darkness dreams the light,
candle light is tender to the night
plays with shadows, leaving

in every corner a mystery
as does this wood, lost in this
the shortest of days,

in the garden a stillness
the air hushed, bent is the hollyhock
bruised the last rose,

do not place stones in my pocket
nor whistle
I hear well enough.

The Seventh of September

Annual sweeping of my cottage chimney,
Autumn already in the air.
Mr Badger my chimney sweep
arrives with rods and brushes,
a gentle shower of soot
on all he touches.
First, we take tea together
inspect with care
my roses, discuss the weather
what wood is best to burn
apple for scent, but only ash
burns fierce when it is green.
Outside I'm sent, my part
to watch for Mr Badger's brush burst
triumphant from the chimney pot
I gather pods of ripe sweet *Lathyrus*
both pink and white,
my gift for Mr Badger, before
I wave him out of sight;
his gift to me, his country lore
"Never burn elder, it draws
the devil down the chimney"
now that's a thing to remember
on for the seventh of September.

Spring Song

In the immense mussel black sky
hanging low over the snow covered barn
a solitary star blazons in the west,

in this cold crisp March air, snow
sparkling the hedge, the earth,
Venus the evening star, heralding the spring.

Echoes

Planting snowdrops, I had found them
at the far end, by the wall.
As I dug the hole, I saw them,
white, against the soil.

In my hand I held them
images, libations
from the past, china
children, one inch long.

Someone once, had loved them,
lost them, some Victorian chid.
Now beside each other, on
my hanging shelves they lie,
votive offerings from the earth.

Sometimes, when the rain is falling
or in the sighing of the leaves
I hear a sound, a child is crying,
calling. Then I need
to plant more snowdrops
at the far end by the wall.

March

Snow covers the ground
fingers of late afternoon sun
brush gold on green black trunks

of beech trees, in a row, opposite
the cottages. Scrawny arms,
branches reaching for a sky

blue as chicory flowers, puffs
of pink corn cockle clouds,
black seeds of beautiful destruction.

Snow outlines the apple tree
a chalk drawing on a child's slate,
slight breeze from the north, worries

frozen leaves, small trees. Footprints
of deer of birds, pattern the whiteness.
Inside the cottage a singing wood fire

crackles, flames throw leaping shadows
in the chimney corner, the only other sound
a clock, tick tocking into spring.

Out of Nowhere

Not sure what I'd seen
out of nowhere
a shadow crossed my window
shook the roses
seizes the small bird,
out of nowhere
came the sparrow-hawk
leaves trembling
petals falling.